What Thou
Lovest Well,
Remains American

By Richard Hugo

What Thou Lovest Well, Remains American

by Richard Hugo

W · W · NORTON & COMPANY · INC ·

NEW YORK

Some of these poems have appeared in the following publications.

American Poetry Review, American Review, Choice, Dacotah Territory, Earth Journal, Field, Gulfstream, Iowa Review, Ironwood, Jeopardy, New American Review, New Letters, Northwest Review, Ploughshares, Poetry Northwest, Quarry, Shenandoah, Poetry Now.

"Approaching the Castle," "Old Scene," and "Indian Girl" originally appeared in *Poetry* © 1973 by the Modern Language Association. "On Hearing a New Escalation" originally appeared in *Poetry* © 1972 by the Modern Language Association. All reprinted by permission of the editor of *Poetry*. "Cattails" originally appeared in *Shenandoah: The Washington and Lee University Review* © 1973 by *Shenandoah*, reprinted with the permission of the editor. "Last Day There" originally appeared in *The New Yorker* © 1974 The New Yorker Magazine, Inc.

Copyright © 1975 by W. W. Norton & Company, Inc.

First Edition

Library of Congress Cataloging in Publication Data

Hugo, Richard F
    What thou lovest well, remains American.

    I. Title.
PS3515.U3W5   811'.5'4   75–4513
ISBN 0–393–04410–6
ISBN 0–393–04417–3 pbk.

1 2 3 4 5 6 7 8 9 0

For Ripley

because no one will mean this much again

Contents

A Snapshot of the Auxiliary

Strangers

Lectures, Soliloquies, Pontifications

A Snapshot of the Auxiliary

A Snapshot of the Auxiliary

In this photo, circa 1934,
you see the women of the St. James Lutheran
Womens Auxiliary. It is easy
to see they are German, short, squat,
with big noses, the sadness of the Dakotas
in their sullen mouths. These are exceptions:
Mrs. Kyte, English, who hated me.
I hated her and her husband.
Mrs. Noraine, Russian, kind. She saved me once
from a certain whipping. Mrs. Hillborn,
Swedish I think. Cheerful. Her husband
was a cop. None of them seem young. Perhaps
the way the picture was taken. Thinking back
I never recall a young face, a pretty one.
My eyes were like this photo. Old.

This one is Grandmother. This my Aunt Sarah,
still living. That one—I forget her name—
the one with maladjusted sons. That gray
in the photo was actually their faces.
On gray days we reflected weather color.
Lutherans did that. It made us children of God.
That one sang so loud and bad, I blushed.
She believed she believed the words.
She turned me forever off hymns. Even
the good ones, the ones they founded jazz on.

Many of them have gone the way wind recommends
or, if you're religious, God. Mrs. Noraine,
thank the wind, is alive. The church
is brick now, not the drab board frame

you see in the background. Once I was alone
in there and the bells, the bells started to ring.
They terrified me home. This next one in the album
is our annual picnic. We are all having fun.

Saying Goodbye to Mrs. Noraine

And after forty years her flowers failed to sing.
Geraniums blanched. Her blue begonias lost
their battle to the dulling rain. The neighborhood
was dead and gone. Only lines of kindness
in her face remained and her remarkable
arbor, my thoughts of wine. I stood clumsy
on her porch and worried if she wondered
why I'd come. When I walked in her door
I knew more secrets than ever about time.

It turned out I remembered most things wrong.
Miss Holy Roller never had
an illegitimate son. The military father
had been good to animals and the Gunthers
were indifferent to Hitler when we stoned
their house. I remembered some things right.
A dog was scalded by hot paraffin.
Two children died and a strange man really lived
alone a block away, shades always drawn,
and when we sang our mocking song about
the unseen man, we really heard him beating walls.

The rest was detail I had missed. Her husband's
agonizing prolonged death. Her plan to live
her last years in another city south.
It was lucky you came, she said. Four days
and I'll be gone. Outside, on the road
the city'd never paved, gravel cracked like popcorn
and everywhere the dandelions adult years
had taught me to ignore told me what I knew

when I was ten. Their greens are excellent
in salad. Their yellow flowers
make good wine and play off like a tune
against salal I love remembering to hum.

A Good Day for Seeing Your Limitations

I wake, birds flashing on my lids. The dead
float off like sullen balloons and I climb
out of dreams where girls swim burgundy,
hair undulating like gills, and into the world
of real air, real firs bending only so far
in the rare morning wind. On page two
of the paper, the hour of sunrise and set.
The forecast is definite: no chance of rain.

The river that splits my town's inflated
near flood. Farms in the lowlands are fearful
and farmers resort to prayer, their cows oblivious
and grand in the pasture. The boy who loses
the fight will play the sneer of the girl
he fought for and lost, deep in his nightmare.
He will die daily in classrooms. He will find
coins in his blood. Obituary ages range
from 10 to 78. I lust over the knees
of the 4-H girls on page nine.

Maybe a coed I almost loved will return
today, to the school, abandoned by her husband,
nerves near storm, words searching my hand.
I have little to give. Just that durable gift
from Michigan, a century old, where a home
burned down and men from neighboring farms
pitched in to build a new one free.
They said, 'Don't worry,' and the dispossessed
stopped weeping and danced to ringing mauls.

The House on 15th S.W.

Cruelty and rain could be expected.
Any season. The talk was often German
and we cried at the death of strangers.
Potatoes mattered and neighbors who came
to marvel at our garden. I never helped
with the planting. I hid in woods these houses
built on either side replaced. Ponds
duplicated sky. I watched my face
play out dreams of going north with clouds.

North surely was soft. North was death
and women and the women soft. The tongue
there was American and kind. Acres of women
would applaud me as I danced, and acres
of graves would dance when sun announced
another cloud was dead. No grating scream
to meals or gratuitous beatings,
no crying, raging fists against closed doors,
twisted years I knew were coming at me,
hours alone in bars with honest mirrors,
being fun with strangers, being liked
so much the chance of jail was weak
from laughter, and my certainty of failure
mined by a tyrant for its pale perverted ore.

My pride in a few poems, my shame
of a wasted life, no wife, no children,
cancel out. I'm left neutral as this house,
not caring to go in. Light would be soft

and full, not harsh and dim remembered.
The children, if there are children inside,
would be normal, clean, not at all
the soiled freaks I had counted on.

A Snapshot of 15th S.W.

Burn this shot. That gray is what it is.
Gray gravel in the street and gray hearts
tired of trying love. Your house:
that ominous gray shake alone on the right,
pear tree bent in what must have been wind
and gray boy playing. The wind had a way
of saying The Lord Is My Shepherd high
in electric wires. That blur could be
a bitter wren or a girl named Mary Jane
running away from a prehistoric father.

The empty lot is where a home burned down.
Shriek of siren. Red on cloud. The suicide.
Every March, the orchard's vivid repair.
The good were quick getting out of here.
For others, the sea, a short mile on the map,
was a long way. Water was tattered
by the time they arrived, shiplanes out
clogged with kelp and debris.

The way out can be wild. Exotic poison
of rose thorn. Raw coyote for lunch.
The longer the gray heart took to teach
the heavier the thicket, the crazier
the plains and small towns. Lovers
forever foreign. Concrete walks replaced
crude cinder trails and cruel men
from another planet found a home.
When women crawled like dogs in the mean
beating sun, your gray blood warmed.

Bleached and tormented by steam,
a bird spiraled out of control.

Don't burn it. That gray is what it was.
Clouds are piling white above the sea
like phrases you believe. Echo of swallow.
Rings from a swallow tick widening
over the river and salmon refusing to mourn.
Deep back, out of camera range
the sun pulses on fields you still might run to,
wind a girl's hand on your ear.

Remember Graham

If we spend our life remembering what we love,
to be sure who we are, Graham endures like ivy.
Even if I were, and I wasn't, the poisoner,
nine dogs to my credit, I still might own by right
of blood the long poplar windbreak by the road.
If I were the bigot who ran the bar, September still
might die forever in the fern. Whatever's sad
about moving away is a replay in the throat
of some old deeper grief we'd rather forget.
Again, my car, not old this time, not burning oil,
dives down the hill I've hoarded twenty years
to Graham. All's improved. Fat dogs doze
in buttercups and the kind author of books
about peach trees waves from his porch.
And things are the same. Poplars sway like early girls
in dream and sun flushes the swallows
who ride thermals wisely into the world
of black dazzle and take their place with the stars.

A History of the Sketch

I learned this from the old: odor of lake
and crayola, odor of grave. Cycle completed
and locked. And that was another air, the one
with glittering kites, the one glittering music
from the dancehall rode across the lake.
Isn't it time again for the band to assemble,
trumpet to sparkle, drum to knock like a heart?
And isn't it time for dark women to jitter
through evening like bats, barely missing,
barely nicking the lake? Or should the first kiss
be the last, life from then on
lonely promise in the reeds where water tries
to lap but soft moss muffles the wash?
The blackbird offers no red wing of friendship
under the chilling cloud. Now, when I sketch
a perch and get the wrong green on his rib
no preacher hounds me to correct the color.
And empty days like these are full of time
to stare the color real until the perch
slips off the sketchpad into the lake
and darts for sedge. Bubbles of his going
bloom along the surface. They give off
definite odors hermits remember well.

Why I Think of Dumar Sadly

Forgive this nerve. I walked here up the long hill
from the river where success is unpretentious commerce,
tugs towing saleable logs and drab factories tooting
reliable workers home. Here, the stores are balanced
on the edge of failure and they never fail. Minimal
profits seem enough to go on one more day
and stores that failed were failures in the '30s.
The district failed from the beginning. The pioneer
who named it for himself died wondering what's wrong
with the location. Three blocks north the houses end.
Beyond them, gravel pits and Scotch broom.

The nerve I ask forgiveness for is in my gaze.
I see this district pale. When lovers pass me
on their way to love I know they'll end up hating
and fresh paint gleaming yellow on the meeting hall
peels before it dries. Whatever effort the grocer
makes to increase sales, he'll end up counting pennies
in a dim room, bewildered by volitant girls
who romp in clouds above his store. The family next door
is moving after thirty years to Phoenix. The well built
daughter of the druggist started sagging yesterday.

I think of Dumar sadly because a dancehall burned
and in it burned a hundred early degradations.
How I never knew the reason
for a girl's wide smile, a blue spot raying over dancers,
a drum gone silent and the clarinet alone. I hear
the sad last shuffling to Good Night Sweetheart. I take
the dark walk home. Now see the nerve you must forgive.
Others in pairs in cars to the moon flashing river.
Me on foot alone, asking what I do wrong.

Time to Remember Sangster

One of us would spot his horse, same white
as his mustache, and word traveled on warm air.
While he solicited orders at doors
we stole pears from his cart, that battered
gray board flatbed held together by luck.
He was obsolete as promise. His apples
felt firm green and his cherries were loaded
with black exploding sun. Those days
seemed ripe as women we expected to meet
under flowering trees when we grew up.

Summer and summer he came, he, the horse
and the cart beyond aging, all three
frozen ninety-two. To children
he was old as tears. We asked him what caused weather.
We asked him about future wars. He sat mute
as orchards abandoned to the heat.
Summer on summer our delighted thieving
went on until he died and summer went void.

They took me to his funeral. Open casket.
I exploded when I saw him, his mustache
touched up blue not looking like it looked,
his eyes shut tight as a canyon wall
of sand. They dragged me into the light.
Days I walked alone our street that empty summer
telling dogs, it's wrong. Thirty-five years later
in England, a place called Enfield, I saw
three white horses in a field so close to town
they seemed to not belong. I decided then
I liked the English. I never thought of him.

Again, Kapowsin

That goose died in opaque dream.
I was trolling in fog when the blurred
hunter stood to aim. The chill gray
that blurred him amplified the shot
and the bird scream. The bird was vague form
and he fell as a plane would fall on a town,
unreal. The frantic thrashing was real.
The hunter clubbed him dead with an oar—
crude *coup de grâce*. Today, bright sky
and the shimmering glint of cloud on black water.
I'm twenty years older and no longer row
for that elusive wisdom I was certain
would come from constant replay of harm.
Countless shades of green erupted up the hill.
I didn't see them. They erupt today, loud
banner and horn. Kingdoms come through for man
for the first time.

This is the end of wrong hunger. I no longer
troll for big trout or grab for that infantile pride
I knew was firm when my hand ran over
the violet slash on their flanks. My dreams include
wives and stoves. A perch that fries white in the pan
is more important than his green vermiculations,
his stark orange pelvic fin. And whatever
I wave goodbye to, a crane waves back
slow as twenty years of lifting fog. For the first time
the lake is clear of hemlock. From now on
bars will not be homes.

Again, Kapowsin. Now the magic is how
distances change as clouds constantly alter

the light. Lives that never altered here are done.
Whatever I said I did, I lied. I did not claw
each cloud that poured above me nude.
I didn't cast a plug so perfectly in pads
bass could not resist and mean faces of women
shattered in the splash. Again, Kapowsin.
The man who claimed he owned it is a stranger.
He died loud in fog and his name won't come.

Flying, Reflying, Farming

We are flying white air. The most pioneering
falcon of all is hopelessly beneath us.
Nothing above but sky bleached out
by the sun's remorseless hammering
through ozone. Our lives inch back below,
the farm gray because a cruel past, weather
or mother, turns the spirit gray. The oldest
daughter left one day for good. The first son
(how can I know this at this altitude)
is trapped for life. At best, he can only get rich.
What good reason could the pilot have
for suddenly pointing the plane at the sun
and cutting the power? I hear his
hysterical laughter all the air down
to rock. We implode into acres
of black we rehearsed every young rage.
Another farm, tiny as the attendant's voice
on the defective intercom slips back
beneath us, bright orange this time and home.
We are flying white air.

The aluminum creaks. The wing shudders.
We are flying rough air. Remember
the wing snapping back over Europe
(where was that?), the agonizing sheer
you saw in slow motion, the vomit
you held back with prayer, and your friend
spinning down fatal ether
man had no business in. Back at the base
you were sobbing fields away from the rest

and the shepherd in black offered you pears
and wouldn't take your money. You claimed
you paid him with tears but that made no sense.
The air is solid again. We eat our way north.
We are flying good air.

We have entered the pattern.
Power reduced. Flaps down. Seat belt sign on.
In a moment, no smoking. This is always
a major kind of return. Thirty years ago
we came down and laughed and shook hands
after a rough one. We congratulated ourselves
for being alive. Long before that
we were ignorant farmers. Remember the night
you came home cheated in town of the money
you'd saved to paint the farm green.
Your wife called you weak and you stammered
and wept. Late one morning years later,
drunk and alone, you remembered above us
air is white, and you knew your next wife
would forgive you, your crops come
fatter than clouds, old friends return.
We have landed on schedule. Reverse thrust.
We are safe. We are natural on earth.

Last Day There

All furniture's gone. It hits me in this light
I've always hated thinned the way it is
by tiny panes, when I leave now the door will slam
no matter how I close it and my groin will throb
hungry as these rooms. Someone left the snapshot
on the wall, two horses and a man, a barn
dark gray against gray light I think was sky
but could be eighty years of fading. Once I called
that unknown farmer friend. He stared back
ignorant and cold until I blushed.
What denies me love today helps me hold a job.

This narrow space I slept in twenty years,
a porch walled in, a room just barely added on.
I own this and I know it is not mine.
That day I found locked doors in Naples, streets
rocked in the sea. The sea rocked in the hands
of brutal sky and fish came raining from volcanoes.
I see the horses swirl into the barn. I hear
two shots, no groans. When I say I'm derelict
the horses will return to flank the farmer.
Again, the three die gray as April 7, 1892.

I'll leave believing we keep all we lose and love.
Dirt roads are hard to find. I need to walk one
shabby some glamorous way the movies like.
I'll rest at creeks. I can't help looking deep
for trout in opaque pools. I pass a farm:
it's home, eviction papers posted to the door,

inside a fat ghost packing wine to celebrate
his fear of quarantine, once outside, pleased the road
he has to take goes north without an exit ramp,
not one sign giving mileage to the end.

Places and Ways to Live

Note the stump, a peach tree. We had to cut it down.
It banged the window every wind. Our garden
swayed with corn each summer. Our crops were legend
and our kindness. Whatever stranger came, we said,
'Come in.' We ran excited. 'Someone's come to see us.'
By night we were exhausted. The dark came early
in that home, came early for the last time soon.

Some nights in motels, I wake bewildered by the room.
Then I remember where I am. I turn the light on
and the girl's still there, smiling from the calendar
whatever the year. When I'm traveling, I'm hurt.
I tune in certain radio stations by heart,
the ones that play old tunes like nothing worthwhile's
happened since that funeral in 1949.

When I'm in the house I've bought, I don't dwell on
the loss of trees, don't cry when neighbors move away
or dogs get killed by cars. I'm old enough to know
a small girl's tears are fated to return, years from now
in some Berlin hotel, though I seem to sit unfeeling
at the window watching it all like a patron.
I'm taking it in, deep where I hope it will bloom.

That is the crude self I've come to. The man who says
suffer, stay poor and I can create. Believe me, friends,
I offer you your homes and wish you well in them.
May kisses rain. May you find warm arms each morning.
May your favorite tree be blooming in December.
And may you never be dispossessed, forced to wander
a world the color of salt with no young music in it.

What Thou Lovest Well,
Remains American

You remember the name was Jensen. She seemed old
always alone inside, face pasted gray to the window,
and mail never came. Two blocks down, the Grubskis
went insane. George played rotten trombone
Easter when they flew the flag. Wild roses
remind you the roads were gravel and vacant lots
the rule. Poverty was real, wallet and spirit,
and each day slow as church. You remember threadbare
church groups on the corner, howling their faith
at stars, and the violent Holy Rollers
renting that barn for their annual violent sing
and the barn burned down when you came back from war.
Knowing the people you knew then are dead,
you try to believe these roads paved are improved,
the neighbors, moved in while you were away, good-looking,
their dogs well fed. You still have need
to remember lots empty and fern.
Lawns well trimmed remind you of the train
your wife took one day forever, some far empty town,
the odd name you never recall. The time: 6:23.
The day: October 9. The year remains a blur.
You blame this neighborhood for your failure.
In some vague way, the Grubskis degraded you
beyond repair. And you know you must play again
and again Mrs. Jensen pale at her window, must hear
the foul music over the good slide of traffic.
You loved them well and they remain, still with nothing
to do, no money and no will. Loved them, and the gray
that was their disease you carry for extra food

in case you're stranded in some odd empty town
and need hungry lovers for friends, and need feel
you are welcome in the secret club they have formed.

Strangers

Goodbye, Iowa

Once more you've degraded yourself on the road.
The freeway turned you back in on yourself
and you found nothing, not even a good false name.
The waitress mocked you and you paid your bill
sweating in her glare. You tried to tell her
how many lovers you've had. Only a croak came out.
Your hand shook when she put hot coins in it.
Your face was hot and you ran face down to the car.

Miles you hated her. Then you remembered what
the doctor said: really a hatred of self. Where
in flashes of past, the gravestone
you looked for years and never found, was there
a dignified time? Only when alone,
those solitary times with sky gray as a freeway.

And now you are alone. The waitress
will never see you again. You often pretend
you don't remember people you do. You joke back
spasms of shame from a night long ago.
Splintered glass. Bewildering blue swirl
of police. Light in your eyes. Hard questions.
Your car is cruising. You cross with ease
at 80 the state line and the state you are entering
always treated you well.

Farmer, Dying

Seven thousand acres of grass have faded yellow
from his cough. These limp days, his anger,
legend forty years from moon to Stevensville,
lives on, just barely, in a Great Falls whore.
Cruel times, he cries, cruel winds. His geese roam
unattended in the meadow. The gold last leaves
of cottonwoods ride Burnt Fork creek away.
His geese grow fat without him. Same old insult.
Same indifferent rise of mountains south,
hunters drunk around the fire ten feet from his fence.

What's killing us is something autumn. Call it
war or fever. You know it when you see it: flare.
Vine and fire and the morning deer come half
a century to sip his spring, there, at the far end
of his land, wrapped in cellophane by light.
What lives is what he left in air, definite,
unseen, hanging where he stood the day he roared.
A bear prowls closer to his barn each day.
Farmers come to watch him die. They bring crude offerings
of wine. Burnt Fork creek is caroling. He dies white
in final anger. The bear taps on his pane.

And we die silent, our last day loaded with the scream
of Burnt Fork creek, the last cry of that raging farmer.
We have aged ourselves to stone trying to summon
mercy for ungrateful daughters. Let's live him
in ourselves, stand deranged on the meadow rim
and curse the Baltic back, moon, bear and blast.
And let him shout from his grave for us.

for Hank and Nancy

28

Living Alone

I felt the empty cabin wasn't abandoned.
The axe, for one thing, blood still moist
on the blade. Then, warm coffee on the stove.
God, it blew outside. The owner, I said,
won't last long in this storm. By midnight
I was singing. I knew the cabin was mine.
Fifty years later, he still hadn't returned.

Moss covered the roof by then. I called
the deer by name. Alice, I liked best.
Winslow, next. Reporters came to write me up.
They called me 'animal man' in the feature
in the photogravure. The story said I led
a wonderful life out here. I said clouds
were giant toads but they quoted me wrong.

The coroner identified the bones as woman.
I denied I'd been married and the local
records backed me. Today, they are hunting all over
the world for the previous owner.
I claim the cabin by occupancy rights.
I pray each dawn. How my words climb cedars
like squirrels uttered by God.

Turtle Lake

The wind at Dog Lake whispered 'stranger' 'stranger'
and we drove away. When we dove down that hill
and flared out on the empty prairie, home seemed
less ashamed of us. My Buick hit a note too high
for dogs at 85 and cattails bowed like subjects
where we flashed through swamp. The wind died
back of us in slipstream. The sky kept chanting
'move like you are moved by water.' When we rolled
into Polson we were clean as kings.

Turtle is a lake the odd can own. It spreads
mercurial around those pastoral knolls.
The water waits so still, we listen to grim planets
for advice. The beat of trout hearts amplifies
against the Mission Range and when that throb returns
our faces glow the color of the lake. This
is where we change our names. Five clouds cross
the sun: the lake has been six colors,
counting that dejected gray our lives brought in.

The old man fishing fills his limit and goes home.
The heron takes his limit: one. All five clouds
poured east to oblivion and from the west advice
is pouring in. This mute wind
deeds the lake to us. Our homes have burned down
back where wind turned hungry friends away.
Whatever color water wants, we grant it with a wave.
We believe this luxury of bondage, the warm way
mountains call us citizens in debt.

for Sena

Late Summer, Drummond

A long freight swims upwind. Each 4 P.M., the river
limps upwind on schedule. Angus doze beneath
the cottonwoods that flare and lean. The town beyond
the pasture, once a speedtrap noted for harsh fines,
now bypassed by I90, bakes the same dead gray
the arm bakes sheered by lightning from the tree.
The red caboose drags west sorry. The town drunk
staggers to the tracks and waves it gone.

With mean traps bypassed, no more fines to pay,
we're free to love the movement east, eastbound trees,
traffic on the freeway. Speed law: safe and sane.
Real speed: blinding. Real chance to make it: none.
Our best chance: love the leaf flash spreading white
above the napping cows. The town drunk knows
the world blurs, drunk or sober, and the world moves on
out of reach against the wind or with.

Boxcars full of cows go west for slaughter.
Underground, seepage from the river
ignites another green. The gray arm left by lightning
turns sheer silver in the rain. Real chance
to make it: none. Life becomes a hobby seen
like this from hills, the empty freight returned.
The town drunk waves goodbye to cars that flash east
safe as cattle when their dreams revive the grass.

for Ellen Skones

Reading at the Old Federal Courts Building, St. Paul

The gavel hammered. The sentence tore my ear
and I went chained, degraded down these halls,
so terrified the letters jittered on the doors:
U.S. Marshal Detention Room; Court of Appeals.
What had I done wrong? The judge was marble.
The young girl witness laughed at all those years
I'd serve in isolation. The pillars smiled.
In my cell, I sobbed vengeance on their world.

That was years back, understand. The first fall
I had taken, the first hint girls might testify
against me all my life because I'm cowardly
and born infirm. And that was the first time
I began to understand my rage, the licensed anger
and resultant shame. Sentence after sentence
I went burning down these halls, flashbulbs
blinding as the prosecution evidence.

The renovation's clearly underway. Today
girls ask me how I started writing. I read
the poems I wrote in jail. Warm applause.
Autographs. Interviews. The judge died lingering
in pain from cancer. That girl who laughed,
first trial, is teaching high school and she
didn't know me when she said she loved my poems,
was using them in class to demonstrate how
worlds are put together, one fragment at a time.

Ode to the Trio Fruit Company of Missoula

See how the red name faded hard to sorry
on the yellow sign, and how the spur along
the loading platform's empty as a hand.
Most of all, listen to the silence, the nothing
that's behind those bolted doors, humming
like a note too old to hear. When Italians
move away, the air hangs silent as a pear.

Knock once. Then crack the frozen bolt with anger.
When plums dried in his dream, the office manager
brought all his energy to work. Inside, we find
the ledgers curled from sweat. The sickening odors
of some former fruit order us to cross the days off
on the calendar and wait, two life term prisoners.
The track stood barren just two days and crows flew north

to Bigfork where the cherries flare. And if, here,
we must face the falling profit, the new way
apples are preserved, the failure of the railroad,
we should also know the vital way birds locate orchards,
we should also fly the stale air of our tiny cell,
poking the corners light ignores. The poor
feed well on those discarded planets they explore.

We are rich as tramps. Even in this gloom
a record shipment gleams and we cry *venga venga*
to a derailed train. In the supermarket
where the light is whole, we can finger lemons
for the right one and the price will ring.
Think how colors ring and how those loud pears climb
in tiers like choirs on display.

for Sarah Wilcox

33

Old Scene

All the essentials were there, the river thin
from distance in the canyon below, the house above
the canyon and the old man pruning trees. Whatever
he felt left out appeared, the carnival band
in step on the dirt road, the road remote enough
to need a name, lovely girls asking directions.
The old man's house was the last one. After that,
the road forever in the sun. He looked down that road
every noon and nothing came—mail or flashing girl.
He needed a dog but that you couldn't provide.

In time you gave him wisdom. A way of knowing
how things are from photos. He stared long enough
to make the photoed live. A farmer told him
pears grew big in '97. Children danced at dawn
and horses, the horses ran and ran. You let him
ride one and you helped him learn which woman
in one picture loved him at the Baptist fair.

You joined him one day at the river. After hours
of trout you walked together up the long slope
where he pointed to his house. He said 'Come in'
and built a fire and you said 'I live here too.'
Some days, the road fills suddenly with clowns.
The carnival band plays every tune you love.
Lovely girls stream in. You are dazzled
by their sequins, and the odor of their cooking
makes you laugh. Other days, the road hangs
empty. Not even birds can raise the dust.

Landscapes

If I painted, I'd paint landscapes. In museums
I stop often at van Ruysdael, and the wind he painted
high in European oaks gives license to my style.
I move the barn two feet. I curve the hill down
more dramatic. I put a woman on the hill against
the light, calling me to dinner. The wind I paint
is low and runs the grass down dancing to the sea.

In no time I have aged the barn stark gray.
Obviously, my cows hate no one. My wife
across the field stays carved out solid on the sky.
My tossed kiss stings her through the waves of heat
plowed dirt gives off in August. My tossed worm
drifts beneath the cutbank where I know trout wait.
As long as wind is pouring, my paint keeps farming green.

When wind stops, men come smiling with the mortgage.
They send me the eviction notice, postage due.
My cows are thin and failing. My deaf wife snarls
and claws the chair. The creek turns putrid.
I said fifty years moss on the roof is lovely.
It rots the roof. Oaks ache but cannot stir.
I call van Ruysdael from my knees on the museum floor.

In uniforms like yours you'll never understand.
Why these questions? The bank was wrong. The farm
is really mine. Even now along these pale green halls
I hear van Ruysdael's wind. Please know I rearranged things
only slightly, barn and hill. This is real: the home
that warps in August and the man inside who sold it
long ago, forgot he made the deal and will not move.

Reconsidering the Madman

To him the window broken in the church
guaranteed oblivion. He ran out naked
in a record winter for Wyoming.
He said nothing's more heroic than a road
curving with the river warm away from farms
like horses curving into fog. He said a road
hardens like a man from weather.

We said good riddance to his crazy chatter.
One year later, we gave the day he left
a number not found on a calendar.
To celebrate the mayor composed a song
about a loving dog who killed ten snakes
to save the mining camp. We sang that loud
around the fire and we mocked the man.

Jokes turned into stories. Suddenly the lyrics
were about the fear of man, that man
most of all. Sweet Nick, we sang, Sweet Nick
(a name we'd given him), come home. The surface
of the river twitched from nerves. Swallows
strafed the trout in terror and when we screamed
old hymns our new church shook and broke.

Maybe he was right, the hope of roads goes on
and on. We found bones we think were him.
If not, why were they raving in the heat
and why would he head any way but south
where early every spring the roads suck blood
from rivers and the first chinook blows in,
blows in lemon and the yellow melts the snow.

The Cripples

Where were they headed, the one winged birds
tilted to compensate, dependent on thermals
to lift them over the mountains, and that annual blast
from the Gulf of Alaska to carry them far as Peru?
They seemed various ages, as much as 4,000 years
separating young from old, and they sang one song
with as many bold variations as throats. Their flight
was song and soaring. Through the county telescope
we saw they were various colors and shapes. Some
had belligerent beaks and others relied on the warmth
of their tints. Each seemed little alone. But when
we zoomed back and scanned, as a group they glowed
like glory children believe. We watched them
burn into dots, into nothing, and turned back
to our plowing as if they never had passed.

Invasion North

They looked soft floating down. White puffs that glowed
in sunlight like dandelion seed. And they landed
softly in the snow, discarded the billowing white silk,
formed squadrons based on types of weapon
and started marching at us, one drum rolling,
armor gleaming on their breasts. We tried to joke
inside the igloo fortress but we timed
the punchlines badly. Finally, the captain said
we'd better load. They were two miles off and closing.

They closed fast. The drum roared loud as cannon.
God, they were big. White uniforms and makeup.
Our mascot polar bear broke his titanium chain
and ran. The last order I remember from the captain
was retreat. I remember being alone. The wind against
my face. The walrus. Flashes on the horizon.
I knew without seeing it our fortress was destroyed.
And I knew somehow the enemy soldiers, those women
in military nylon had beaten us. I cried.

Of the entire garrison, I am the only survivor.
Lord, it's cold, wandering this ice alone. My radio
still works. The conquering women have offered me
the captain's skeleton, have promised amnesty
if I come in. They broadcast every day at noon
and again at nine on clear nights. They must think
I'm a fool. I've developed a terrible arsenal
in case I'm taken and I've stockpiled berries,
roots and dry meat, enough to last fifty years.

Cattails

It's what I planned. The barbershop alone
at the edge of Gray Girl swamp, the town beyond
drowsing that battering raw afternoon,
the radio in the patrol car playing westerns,
the only cop on duty dreaming girls.
When I walked in, first customer, the barber
muttered 'Murder' and put his paper down.
I hinted and hinted how sinister I am.
The barber said 'I'm sorry' when he cut my ear.

This is where I'd planned the end, in cattails
and cold water, my body riddled, face down
in the reeds, hound and siren howling red,
camera popping, the barber telling the reporter
what I'd said. And wind. Always wind that day,
bending the cattails over my body, bringing cloud
after cloud across the sun and in that shifting light
women whispering 'Who was he?,' and the cop
trying to place me, finding my credit cards,
each with a fictitious foreign name.

When my hair was cut, I walked along the bank
of Gray Girl swamp and watched the cattails rage.
When I drove out, my radio picked up the same lament
the cop had on. I tuned in on his dream.
They came to me, those flashing, amber girls,
came smiling in that wind, came teasing laughter
from my seed like I'd done nothing wrong.

The Hilltop

I like bars close to home and home run down,
a signal to the world, I'm weak. I like a bar
to be a home. Take this one. Same men every night.
Same jokes. Traffic going by
fifteen feet away and punchboards never paying off.
Churn of memory and ulcer. Most of all
the stale anticipation of the girl
sure to walk in someday fresh from '39,
not one day older, holding out her arms.

Soon, I say to no one late each night,
I'll be all right. I put five dollars
in the jukebox and never hear a tune.
I take pride drinking alone and being kind.
When I walk in, people say my name.
By ten, the loveliest girl in Vegas
swims about the room, curving in and counter
to the flow of smoke. Her evil sister
swings her legs and giggles in my drink.

When I'm at home, the kitchen light stays on.
Help me, friend. By dawn, a hundred dogs
are gnawing at my throat. My gnarled phlegm
chokes up yellow. My empty room
revolves tornado and my relatives
are still unnamed. A dozen practiced gestures
get me through the day. By five, I'm crawling
up the hill, certain I'll live, my Hilltop smile
perfected and my coin naïve.

for Susan Zwinger

Changes in Policy at Taholah

They're denying whites the beach. The tribe says
no more casting for perch in the surf. No fires.
No walks under the moon. My instinct says we have done
much harm. The sea says nothing. The sea
has a violent way of cleaning the sand.

Be easy, wind and tide. The river's cringing this close
to the end. Ospreys dive to doom the salmon
or to doom. The undertow removes the bones
of preying fathers and in death the sea bass
pale out placid gray from black.

Even Indians pale. Spray flung wild as arteries
keeps draining human color.
The chief is white and dying.
Silhouettes of firs are black spears every dawn.
Bluebacks caught in tribal nets are sweating.

The ocean has the last word on possession.
The more threatening the day, the wilder
water's laughter. It leaves us sand to die on
and it leaves the bones it took twelve hours
every twenty-four before it takes them back.

Consider this a cry against the sea, S. J.
Grant the tribe its right to keep us out.
We'll get there anyway, even if we have to slant our route
like seabirds in, ranting on the downwind leg alive
on what the sea provides.

for S. J. Marks

Indian Girl

Days she looks at floors, a thick degrading cloud
crosses her face for minutes and I think of wheat.
And in what must have been slow days, I see a girl
packing dirt like makeup, preparing herself for years
of shacks and drunks, stale air filling morning
and the fire out, grease a soapy gray in pots.
You need a blind wild faith in crazy neighbors,
in rocket ships one plans to build for children,
the flight you will be taking in and out of stars.

Stars are not in reach. We touch each other
by forgetting stars in taverns, and we know
the next man when we overhear his grief. Call the heavens
cancerous for laughs and pterodactyls clown
deep in that fragmented blue. In that red heart
a world is beating counter to the world.
My sweet drum, be silent. War paint's running
down her face two centuries of salt. My skin
is bland. My pain can be explained away in bars.

Bad rains, I look for her. Look deep in reeds along
the stagnant ponds and deep in desperate ends
of boxcars. Someday, I'll find her huddled
fighting back the cold with tongues. My strong teal,
please know these words attend you always. Know years ago
long before you lived, I prayed for power of mind
to break these rigid patterns of the nerve.
And should it come, don't think I won't walk miles
of barren rails to touch you like a daughter.

for Bobbi

The Swimmer at Lake Edward

He was crude as a loon on land. His tongue
drove girls away and he sat in taverns hours
and the fat piled up. Women and children
mocked him when he waddled home. Alone
in his rented room he made friends
with the wall and chair. He dialed Time
to hear a voice, and when the voice said 4 A.M.,
he said, no, that couldn't be the time.

He lost jobs fast. In interviews he blushed
and took the menial: watchman on the freights,
raking the ingot yard in the mill,
sweeping halls in the posh insurance firm.
He felt warm alone in his mind, no one
about and light cut in half by cloud
or a shortage of power. And he sang alone
in his mind, tunes he connected with rain.

The first warm day, he dove from the sky
into the lake we named for the king. We stood
on the shore and marveled at his wake.
When we applauded, he flashed away,
his dorsal fin the only point in the glare.
What was his name? We took home the salad
left over but forgot one blanket, a thermos
and the baby's favorite toy.

Ghost in a Field of Mint

The old man on the prison work release gang
hoeing asphalt followed us to Wilkeson
and those cyrillic graves, to Carbanado
and that one long empty street, Voight's Creek
and then Kapowsin and our picnic
in a field of mint. Wherever we went, old haunts
I wanted you to see, he hung there grim.
I ruined him with theory: sodomy, infanticide.
His bitter face kept saying we die broken.
Our crab paté seemed bitter and the sun.

In old poems I put evil things in Carbanado
where I'd never been because a word that soft
and lovely must be wrong, must hide what
really happened, the unreported murder
in the tavern, faithless wives. Clouds were birds
of prey. The cell door clangs before we know
we're doing wrong. The stern click of the calendar
damned us long ago to take pain on the tongue.

One day, alone in an asylum, I will find
a door left open and the open field beyond,
a wife beside that road the map forgot
waiting as prearranged.
She'll say, I'm crazy too. I understand.
From then on we will seek the harboring towns,
towns you never find, those flowers dying
certain the forlorn die wise. My sister,
we have been released for the entire day.

for Sister Madeline DeFrees

Iowa Déjà Vu

Did I come from this, a hardware store
in photos long ago? No customers.
No pleasures but the forced dream pike
are cruising hungry in the lake that glows
through oaks a small walk from the farm.
The church I must attend, hard dirt and plow,
sweating horse I swear at, all the hate
that makes today tomorrow.
Next farm down the daughters married Germans.
Girls don't like me in the town.

West of here love is opportune.
I get this from the soft cry of a train;
from magazines the barber lets me take.
West, it cools at night. Stars reproduce
like insects and wild horses sing.
Here it's planting time and never harvest,
nothing but the bitterest of picnics,
the camera just invented and in first prints
women faded and the children old.

Morning again. Morning forever. The heat
all night all day. The day of sweat
and heat forever and the train gone on.
It's where I began, first choking
on a promise to be nice, first dreaming pike
were hungry in the lake I didn't try.

The Freaks at Spurgin Road Field

The dim boy claps because the others clap.
The polite word, handicapped, is muttered in the stands.
Isn't it wrong, the way the mind moves back.

One whole day I sit, contrite, dirt, L.A.
Union Station, '46, sweating through last night.
The dim boy claps because the others clap.

Score, 5 to 3. Pitcher fading badly in the heat.
Isn't it wrong to be or not be spastic?
Isn't it wrong, the way the mind moves back.

I'm laughing at a neighbor girl beaten to scream
by a savage father and I'm ashamed to look.
The dim boy claps because the others clap.

The score is always close, the rally always short.
I've left more wreckage than a quake.
Isn't it wrong, the way the mind moves back.

The afflicted never cheer in unison.
Isn't it wrong, the way the mind moves back
to stammering pastures where the picnic should have worked.
The dim boy claps because the others clap.

Lectures, Soliloquies, Pontifications

Plans for Altering the River

Those who favor our plan to alter the river
raise your hand. Thank you for your vote.
Last week, you'll recall, I spoke about how water
never complains. How it runs where you tell it,
seemingly at home, flooding grain or pinched
by geometric banks like those in this graphic
depiction of our plan. We ask for power:
a river boils or falls to turn our turbines.
The river approves our plans to alter the river.

Due to a shipwreck downstream, I'm sad to report
our project is not on schedule. The boat
was carrying cement for our concrete rip rap
balustrade that will force the river to run
east of the factory site through the state-owned
grove of cedar. Then, the uncooperative
carpenters union went on strike. When we get
that settled, and the concrete, given good weather
we can go ahead with our plan to alter the river.

We have the injunction. We silenced the opposition.
The workers are back. The materials arrived
and everything's humming. I thank you
for this award, this handsome plaque I'll keep
forever above my mantle, and I'll read
the inscription often aloud to remind me
how with your courageous backing I fought
our battle and won. I'll always remember
this banquet this day we started to alter the river.

Flowers on the bank? A park on Forgotten Island?
Return of cedar and salmon? Who are these men?

These Johnnys-come-lately with plans to alter the river?
What's this wild festival in May
celebrating the runoff, display floats on fire
at night and a forest dance under the stars?
Children sing through my locked door, 'Old stranger,
we're going to alter, to alter, alter the river.'
Just when the water was settled and at home.

Three Stops to Ten Sleep

Ho. The horses can water. We are miles
ahead of schedule thanks to cool weather
and a strong wind at our backs. Ahead
are the mountains where we plan to build
our city. Our bank will be solvent. Our church
will serve all faiths. We will pass tough laws
against fragmentation. Anyone threatening
unity will be sent to the plains to wander
forever. The plains have snakes and wolves
and much of the water is poison. Have the women
make dinner. We camp here. Tomorrow
we should be close to that forest, and the next day
we will find our place to live as destined.

Stop. It is farther than it seemed. No doubt
an illusion created by light off high snow.
Then, the wind changed and discouraged
the horses. They don't like wind full in their eyes
all day. I urge you to stop this bickering.
Remember, our city will be founded
on mutual respect. I urge you to accept
this necessary rationing of food.
Above all, remember, every time you frown
the children see it. Several already
have been crying and saying there will be no city.

Wait. The mountains are never closer. What
is this land? We lost too many last night
in the storm and those who remain
are the worst, the ones we hesitated to take
when we started back at the river. You

51

remember? That town where we first formed?
Those saloons and loose women? Let them grumble.
We are going on. Indians know
the right roots to eat and there's water in cactus.
Even if we fail, wasn't it worth the trip,
leaving that corrupting music behind
and that sin?

On Hearing a
New Escalation

From time one I've been reading slaughter,
seeing the same bewildered face of a child
staring at nothing beside his dead mother
in Egypt, the pyramid blueprints approved,
the phrases of national purpose streaming
from the mouth of some automated sphynx.
Day on day, the same photographed suffering,
the bitterness, the opportune hate handed down
from Xerxes to Nixon, a line strong
as transatlantic cable and stale ideals.
Killing's still in though glory is out of style.
And what does it come to, this blood cold
in the streets and a history book printed
and bound with such cost-saving American
methods, the names and dates are soon bones?
Beware certain words: Enemy. Liberty. Freedom.
Believe those sounds and you're aiming a bomb.

Announcement

Tomorrow morning at four, the women will be herded
into the public square to hear their rights read aloud.
I'm pleased to sign this new law. No longer
will women be obliged to kneel and be flayed
by our southern farmers. This law says, farmers
must curb their mean instincts. From now on
women as well as men they use country water.

I'm sorry the farmers grumble. A way of life
is passing. But good things remain. The sun
still cares for the land. We still have our chant
that seduces rain in July. And women's tears
at the wonderment of tide will always be legal,
reminding us over and over of their depth of feeling.
Our laws have always respected women.

Let me remind you, by law we don't own the sea.
Only our Gods, the clouds, own salt water.
Our Bill of Rights simply assumes we may troll
Their blue property for pollack and mackerel.
When the clown-devil Nimbus plays dark tricks out
on the sea, claiming an occasional boat,
we pray to Cumulus, and He rumbles in thought.

In our wisdom we change what can be changed
and leave the other alone. We don't play around
with those inviolate structures of wind
that pile the souls of our ancestors high
on the evening horizon in luminous banks of gold
and the basic right we all have to die.
We grant stars what is theirs and fight misery.

For Jennifer, 6, on the Teton

These open years, the river
sings 'Jennifer Jennifer.'
Riverbeds are where we run to learn
laws of bounce and run.
You know moon. You know your name is silver.

The thought of water locked tight in a sieve
brings out the beaver's greed.
See how violent opaque runoff moves.
Jennifer, believe
by summer streams come clean for good.

Swirl, jump, dash and delirious veer
become the bright way home
for little girl and otter
far from the punishing sun,
games from organized games.

This river is a small part of a bigger.
That, another.
We get bigger and our naming song gets lost.
An awful ghost
sings at the river mouth, off key.

When you are old and nearing the sea,
if you say this poem
it will speak your name.
When rivers gray,
deep in the deepest one, tributaries burn.

Approaching the Castle

The riches we find inside will be in rich light
pulsing off walls of gold. For every man,
at least two girls, banquets featuring
Yugoslavian tuna in spiced tomato oil
and roasted Kashmir pig. A Sicilian liqueur
will leave us clear the morning after.
In the moat, five pound cutthroat trout,
no limit, no license required, a bait
that always works. In our excitement
we feel wind spurring our horses. The towers
ride high above us like orchestrated stars.

The drawbridge is down, the gate unguarded,
the coat of arms on the wall faded from rain.
Why is entry so easy? Why no sound?
We were told the court band plays heart thumping jazz
and clowns imported from France make laughter
a legend. Best we circle the castle
and think. Word was, the king would greet us
at the gate and roses shower from minarets.
We would ride in to trumpets and applause.

This winter, many have fallen. Supplies
are low. Those who came down with fever
headed back home. The governor sent word.
He advised us to go in, take notes and send back
a full report. We held several meetings
in the swamp and talked about entering.
Once, we decided to try it but stopped short,
intimidated somehow by the banner
saying 'Welcome,' one side
loose in wind and slapping stone.

Listen, Ripley

We quit that road of sad homes long ago.
Rain, too. That land lay better unmined
in our past. Pale gray fanatics died
like trout in mud. The cruel man on the corner
turned purpler than dawn. His wife became
a carving in the artifact museum. Recall, love,
how we set direction in our jaws and walked away
unafraid of roses. I still believe
the mother screaming 'Don't come back' was mine.

Wolverines we heard back home were mean
fell in beside us and we issued names for them
to use in the parade. There, in that land of banners
even obtuse statements of the local hermit
fluttered from the poles. Dawn came crawling
peach on high snow first, then lemon over wheat.
Hearts were checked for secrets at the door.
Those with none, you and I and some odd creature
from the prairie, sang noon free of charge.

We've been long in this country and we know the tongue.
As for sad homes, they were torn down.
Some nights, between two kisses I remember
some raw degradation in a gravel pit.
Remember sweat and blush and one old woman
in her shack alone, eyes
at her clouded pane converting shade of dead fern
on her weeds to lover. Remember how we shouted
when we passed her home 'Hang in there' going out.

Graves in Queens

How long will these graves go on?
How long will my head ache from
that who's-for-loving booze?
Things went well until—but then
time's a damn sad thing—
time and the time it brings—
selection of a casket
in the mid-price range.

God knows I've curbed responses
in response to current trends
and practiced automatic ones.
Secretaries think I'm nice
except that one, but she—
This curve shows the cost of love
went up in late November
and where it intersects this line
representing the rate of pain
we call point kiss. A damn sad thing.
The stones go on and on.
Caskets must be touching underground.

Now we're welcome at the homes
of those who never spoke before.
Whee. Success. Money coming in.
Welcome at the homes of grovelers
I'm sure. Pigeons I have fed
found better pickings at the dump.
Molding apricots. The faded sign.
Big Lil. Dancer. On at nine.
Eleven. One. Last show. Last gala

strip-down strip-off strip-skin
show with count 'em twenty
gorgeous straight from Vegas and
above all clean cats on at three.
                    A damn sad thing.

From my room, a splendid view
of a statue of a stuffy man
who founded Uruguay, a land
I don't believe in although maps
still show it red below Brazil.
Should I say with noble waving
of my arms I'm free? Ah, liberty.
A gasper goo among nonentities.
A bone the dogs are tossing
to the dogs. Big Lil was a cat.
I believe in Paraguay, Peru.
It's the P that makes them real.
The U that starts out Uruguay
is not a P. UP. United Press.
                    A damn sad thing.

I never told you. Greenland floats.
Is often Africa when no one looks.
Has been Russia in its time and France.
Is never Italy because of snobbery.
I believe in Greenland. It's the G.
Gee. I'd give the world to see
that old gang of mine. A damn
sad bunch of damn sad things.
Lynn is less one eye in Singapore.
Winslow waits behind the door
that opens only at his feeding time,
a time time's sure to bring.

Last night what poem was it where
Joe Langland brought so many birds
down stone dead through the air?
And where did Claire McAllister
get such blond hair? And still
the graves go on. In Mukilteo,
Washington, the graveyard holds
twenty, maybe, all who died
as I recall by 1910.

I'll not die of course. My health
is perfect. I'll admit the jet
we're on our way to get
might crash in Iowa,
I smoke too much, and once
when thirteen at a seance
a spirit scared me half-to-death
forecasting I'd be killed
by rain. Such a damn sad thing.
And I'll select my casket
in the mid-price range.

The bus and graves go on. Millions—
and the lines of stone all point our way.
A damn sad thing. Let's go home to bed.
You didn't mean a thing when you were living
and you don't mean nothing now you're dead.

The morning after a reading
at the YMHA Poetry Center

Starting Back

We were set once. When it rained, each man
got uniformly wet and our curses
rolled uniform over the plains.
Scarcely room for deviation or hope.
Each thing had one name. We aged unnoticed
by the day, exchanging only slightly
differing versions of our common fantasy.
Then, the mutant horses, sudden anger
of cow and glass, three-legged robins.
From that time on we put up houses.

That was (still is) when we started dying.
Windows got bigger. We made bigger curtains.
We stopped begging, took odd jobs
that paid well in vegetables and flesh.
One of us, whoever, invented the stove.
Another, love. Then our gradual discovery
of seasons, four names accounting
for the way trees looked, the relative warmth
of the wind. Copper in time. Tin. Gold.
After that, only some of us seemed right.

On beaches now we wonder what to do
about the vanishing dogfish. In hallways
we have learned to say hello, wear clothes
others approve of or cloth to irritate.
Some of us are starting back, tearing down
the factories, designing on purpose
flimsy tents. It will take long. Dragons
in the hills and sensual cousins wait

at the end. Someday, we will know for sure
we are alone. The world is flat
and the urge in the groin comes at 4 P.M.
Shoes are the last thing we will abandon.

Keokuk

Sky was glowering so thick that day in Keokuk
I knew none of us is loved. The town seemed
one long mill. The mill seemed old as mountains,
dark alps I remember in the war, dim air
full of bombers and the land beneath
a map of land from altitude.
The color made me cold. The homes that nothing
I was certain happened in stood mute so long
I imagined bad things happened in some mind.

I'm sure I saw a river there. I always am.
Even in desert where the parched town stands
abandoned to a spatial flow. If my
memory hoards decrepit boats it also still loves
clustered salmon climbing the Duwamish foggy dawn.
I hear the salmon roll the air and slip
back in. I hear the lost tug tooting 'help'
at Alki Point. When high tide creaks, the ray
of hope piles up like seawalls in the fog.

My Montana plates are signals. Yes, it's true
about the hunting. Better still, the mountains
wild with names. My favorite range: The Crazies.
Mad land opens where you run. Your gaze
must give the rescue team a chance to grow
on the horizon, framed in gold. How eagles
shift above me in the canyons. How Indians
remind me of the cattails I once fashioned
into arrows. I shot them at a friend and hid.

Listen, friends in war, dear salmon, dear old friends,
batter the factory down and live with famine,

your light heads cruising through the rubble,
Keokuk destroyed by bad prayers in the raid.
I've toured Seattle postwar days like this,
the districts indistinct, the aged girls giving way
to teen-age duplicates, my hair the color
I was frightened of in war. The ones who died
ride with me. They sing raw anthems you can't hear.

Topographical Map

Good morning. The horses are ready. The trail
will take us past the final alpine fir
to women so rare they are found only above
the snow line. Even high altitude trout,
the California Golden, find them exciting.
Flowers bloom so colorful there the colors
demand a new spectrum, and wolves turned yellow
in that arid atmosphere howl like angels
every dawn. You have a question? The region
was discovered by pioneers who floated
their findings on stars down to the flats.

If you stay a week in that dry dispassionate air
your thoughts go dreamy. Girls you like best
drift in the sky to music. When they hover
close enough to touch the music gets loud.
Young, you loved those tunes. Old, you will love
those odd breaks in time when memory sings
in your groin and girls in pairs are replayed
fighting like cats for your love, on clouds
in the valleys below. You'll ride those times
higher than song and magic arrow, and ride
the avalanche down to withering routine.

You were coward going in.
Nothing has changed. Alpine fir has all
but disappeared in our blinding progress.
The rest was infantile mouthing. I'm coward too.
The original settlers left no record but tears.
They wept on earth where it counts. They pointed
a vague hand west and we took it from there,

and here's where we are. If I were strong
I'd call those horses out again. The real
is born in rant and the actor's gesture.
Good morning. The horses are ready. The souls
of unique animals and girls above the moisture
wave hello when you come into view.

My Buddy

This then buddy is the blue routine.
You chased a fox one noon.
She hid in a golden rain.
You ran through the gold until
a rainy chill.
If that's it buddy it's a bleak routine.
What happened to you there
may never happen again.

So say buddy it is a bleak routine.
The word caves in your skull.
All eyes give you chill.
The fox shows up on the moon
on the horizon, laughing you blind
painting the routine orange.
What happens to you now
happens again.

Say you deserve it. That's a good routine.
I'm nothing, see,
to the storming worms.
The fox died warm in ground.
Now she's gone tell what a bitch she was
loud in a red routine
and say it never happened to you.
Don't show no pain.

Sweet dear buddy it's a gray routine.
A girl rode in off the prairie
a very snuggly cuddly
had a neat twitch coming in

ran off with another man.
Sorry buddy for the brute routine.
For you it can never happen
over and over again.

One rain more and glory afternoon
complete with gin
and trees gone nuts in the gale
that's always whipping even in heat
when you sweat like the dog you are
when you sweat and swear at me buddy
in my underwear
hoping I have your hair.

Boogie boogie buddy. Scarey boo.
Here's a foxy ghost for you.
One with a heart big as a smirk
and a hot toe in your ear.
You're still my buddy
aren't you?
Sorry. A bizarre machine.
Stay away from my gears.

Hell old buddy back to the routine.
I mean routine routine.
The time clock tied to your dong.
The same bitch punching your card
that very snuggly cuddly
off with another man.
Someday buddy you'll say the wrong thing.
We'll never be friends again.

What to do blue buddy now you're gone?
Sing a song? Sing of a lost routine?
Buddy on skins and me in my cups
crying play it, play it again.

No sense losing a tear to the floor
with a mug of beer in your hand
and the blind proprietor yelling
go on, buddy, go on.

The Art of Poetry

The man in the moon was better not a man.
Think, sad Raymond, how you glare across
the sea, hating the invisible near east
and your wife's hysteria. You'll always be here,
rain or gloom, painting a private Syria,
preferred dimensions of girls. Outside, gulls
scar across your fantasy. Rifled spray on glass
unfocuses the goats you stock on the horizon,
laddering blue like dolphins, looping over the sun.
Better the moon you need. Better not a man.
Sad Raymond, twice a day the tide comes in.

Envy your homemade heroes when the tide is low,
laughing their spades at clams, drinking a breezy beer
in breeze from Asia Minor, in those far far
principalities they've been, their tall wives elegant
in audience with kings. And envy that despairing man
you found one morning sobbing on a log,
babbling about a stuffed heart in Wyoming.
Don't think, Raymond, they'd respond to what's
inside you every minute, crawling slow as tide.
Better not tell them. Better the man you seem.
Sad Raymond, twice a night the tide comes in.

Think once how good you dreamed. The way you hummed
a melody from Norway when that summer storm
came battering the alders, turning the silver
underside of leaves toward the moon. And think,
sad Raymond, of the wrong way maturation came.
Wanting only those women you despised, imitating
the voice of every man you envied. The slow walk